Postscripts

by

By Renée K. Nicholson

Wild Ink Publishing

ISBN: 978-1-958531-77-8 (Paperback)
　　　978-1-958531-78-5 (Ebook)

For Nate: I miss you.

(1976-2019)

Table of Contents

Postcards to West Virgina

I left wild, wonderful.
Sometimes when I travel
through the Midwest I get
flatness headaches. Still, I have flirted
with that region so many years.

A trip to Kentucky and then Ohio,
still in Appalachia, but not you,
I looked for your features,
drove the broken-dreams highway:
mountains stripped, shuttered motels, abandoned
equipment, hillside graveyard
flanked by evergreens. I'd say, I'll be home
soon. Did I ever leave?

Maybe I told you
I was once a dancer? It wouldn't make much
difference. The pirouettes are gone
along with all my soaring leaps. The trees start
their burst of color: chassé, pas de bourrée,
glissade, grand jeté. Now, a certain dreamscape.

We passed your prison, your
Palace of Gold, white peacock
deceased. We passed into Pennsylvania
until we passed back into you, a fickle
lover who returns after the affairs.

Zen Cancer Saloon

--title after D.C. Berry

In the Zen Cancer Saloon
you won't find Clark Gable
nor John Wayne. No six shooters
nor swinging wood doors. The drinks
are damn near poison, drop steady
like a soaking rain. The patrons
readily offer up their stories
like a platter of fried chicken,
side of okra, another of collard greens,
stuff they no longer eat. A shot
of whiskey just to settle the stomach.
Complaints are few at the Zen Cancer Saloon,
& if the fare is noxious, the service, pretty good.
A smile a kind of currency, the tips not bills
nor coins: Gonna lick this thing. Better laugh
than cry. Que sera sera. Every day's a gift
even on the drip. The one place where it'd be okay
to bitch & moan, but the patrons never waiver,
line up at their recliners as if barstools, trade in
happiness, list the things they're grateful for, and slip
into that stupor of not-quite slumber, the racket fading,
last call, tab closed out.

Graffiti Church

Nelly y familia, a thin,
sketched heart
among the other prayers
etched and marked,
on a not-yet restored alcove.
The church for locals, for tourists—
we attend unwashed.
Holy men in Cossacks
chant in Latin,
a woman crosses herself.

I am an interloper, lost,
scribbling in a book,
staring into gold.
Services conclude, the blessing
past, people file out of wooden pews.

I'm cast
into the darkened street,
the blustery night, just as I found
the rhythm of my scattershot dreams,
sprayed doodles over my slow-waltz
heartbeat, not stoic as prophets
or disciples. What magic might
we all believe in? Inside, the silent
graffiti prayers
inch their way heavenward.

Curtain Call

The pain behind the patella radiates
like light through a diamond, colorless,
the lock-jawed silence of stillness
points of princess-cut stone on the soft pulp
of connective tissue. Remember
how you were once beautiful, icy,
like the city after December's decadence &
finery. The clear cold of lake-effect
snow, the steel exoskeleton of covered
over-street crosswalks. Of course, the Pabst,
drafty cool, plush velvet cushions pillowed
a thousand glass slippers. Folds of the heavy curtain
pocket memories like the dust bunnies under
the couch, the uneven wood floor—
not home yet. Wings of aches:
ankles, hips, lower backs. Those old ropes
maneuver the scenery where hurt &
love & sweat hover above the pit—
plucked strings, your ligaments & tendons.
The snow heaps outside, cold and heat fuse,
frothy breath like the head on a pint of beer
bottled in the city's bricked heart. The bus
lumbers and knee twitches, past
the family apartments over
groceries, the smell of halupkis, dance
hall filled with old-fashioned polka,
past the closed frozen custard stand,

skirting the angry, ice-crusted lake.
The smooth vinyl beneath you, scanning
the flat northern town as if there were
answers, or even clues. The stars are not
gems, but the moon's shine cleaves
the dark swath of sky over this town
named for natives long gone. So too, your
last stop, that lamppost where you depart.

Dreamland

My father dreams of West Virginia, his boyhood
on Granddad's farm, hunting dogs baying &
tomatoes in the garden. Now he's tucked
between other mountains and a man-
made lake. We dream as not to die
and when my father dreams, it's not coal
or mines shuttered, not abandoned towns
or JC Penny's turned into a senior center,
not heroin or oxy. He fished streams. Gutted,
cooked, and ate what he caught. He rolled
through, what passed for highways
in a Triumph TR3
bought with money from News & Sentinel
routes. Listened to the Pirates take the series
on a radio set on the chrome-edged table.
Now rusted. Fiestaware chipped. But Dad,
maybe this is the only place we belong.
A broken place, with its ragged side
of the heart. Today I saw a man with an enormous
suitcase. He dragged it down and out
of town. What treasure might require such effort?
In West Virginia, I bought an old house I fill
with oddities and books. Like my father's dreams
I live almost heaven imperfect, so close I might have touched
the night as it pulled across the sky, a dark curtain. The sun
eases through the threadbare spots; it slits and frays soon enough.

Sanctuary of Hearts

So many open,
pierced, of course
women or saints all. Blue
silk-framed faces, wary glances
heavenward. The disciples &
the prophets in downward
repose, men who cannot meet
martyred eyes. The center
heart, crossed, hovers above
a marble altar, exposed & bleeding,
sacrificed. Sorrows, ritual by which
of all us sinners, here
and yet to repent. Simple
wooden pews cannot contain
us, cannot cradle our hearts,
cannot cup all of our delight
and shame. The refracted light
rainbow on the stone,
blood pumping through
the pulpy valves
not with feeble hope,
but with quiet mercy.

Eucalyptus

Nate had a stuffed koala bear that had no name.
As kids, we went to the metro zoo to see
the koala exhibit. In the eucalyptus tree the animal
napped. Heavy-lidded, Nate snoozes.
Chemo works its alchemy—
and Nate is a koala, sleeping
twenty-three hours a day, slipping
from that slumber into a semi-lucid wakefulness
focused on consumption of calories.
Eucalyptus works as both sustenance and drug,
the koala both full and stoned, ears alert to predator
or whatever koalas might fear, hidden within
the tree's leaves. Nate's wrapped in an afghan
our mother crocheted to keep her worried hands busy.
Chemo's a constant drip, not the hour or so of gorging leaves.
Down under, koalas live among the other marsupials;
Down under, the patients stay tethered by tubes to trees
of fluid packs and monitors, all drowsy like koalas perched
in branches, the rhythmic pass of sleep-breathing, eyes shuttered,
hands clasped together as if in some kind of prayer.

Boy Killed on the Grafton Road

Drive-in closed for years,
blank screen shrouded by dusk
pushed against hills, tucked in the crook
of a valley.

Fifty-five miles per hour,
turns, thirty-five, and it's all turns
the way roads wind through West Virginia.
Signs only remind us how safe
we'll never be.

His middle school didn't close.
In ten years, who will remember
one boy's favorite color, what
book he was reading? Dim stars
illuminate that dingy screen, wind-
flickered ghost boys, scenes we'll never know,
just shadows across that gray-matter expanse.
Empathy is all we got, and never

enough. Fall showers, cold rain
collecting in steel barrels, pooling
in clogged gutters, damp earth,
night sweats, moon dipping into the black
pavement, the black sky, that impenetrable quiet.

Virgin of the Americas

Here, a virgin in the sky
watching the city spread,
wingspan across marble sky.
Homes hug the hillside,
a lopsided layer cake.
I gaze over high rises & autos,
a city I don't quite know
except the twisting
roads like West Virginia,
the hairpin turns and spots
where the guardrail's knocked out.
Later, after the cloak of night
shrouds the plaza, the gurgle
of fountain water ushers
a new bride and groom.
Nuptial photos, and I amble
past, both watching and trying
not to intrude, wondering if our virgin
hovering above us is watching
protecting us from
what's in the dark.

Bury the Lead

They say the sharks came early
and stayed late, unwanted guests
off the shores of California because
the early warming of the water,
perhaps caused by El Niño. Who knows?
We're not allowed to utter climate change
anymore. I watch the gathered juvenile great whites
cruise the rocky shoreline via embedded
video. Safe in Appalachian mountains, they say
there are no sharks here. Last week,
while teaching ballet to little girls
a great white SUV careened towards
the glass door of our studio, stopped
inches before crashing through. When
asked, they say that SUV was struck
by an oncoming vehicle that pushed
the great white right up to the clear glass,
driven by a man trying to drive
and shoot up. His severed bumper shoved
in the back seat, the syringe
blood-tinged, left bare and open,
a creepy souvenir. The car
sped away. I've heard all
about the opioid crisis. Nothing
else to do. Here it was,
up close, nearly crashing through. Out west,
great whites patrol the beaches. They say sharks

prefer seals, but perhaps the hapless sea bathers
might choose to call it a day. Lifeguards
fly the flag: waters unsafe. But here—
the patrol acts different. A cop on the scene
did not bag the evidence, threw
the syringe into a Long John Silver's dumpster
among the remnants of fish sandwiches. Blood's
no good, he said, because there's no database
to match it. They say sharks smell blood for miles,
but there are no sharks in Appalachia. We might say
we've manufactured our own kind of predator. Dead
in the water, or on the hillside parking lot,
it doesn't matter much. Let me tell you:
there will be blood
and all kinds of sharks will find it.

Dinner at Pla, Barcelona

Assembled guests—
invited by chance, gathered
along a tabletop where the wine
flows freely as the Besos River:
flirty hellos, bite-sized compliments,
just a taste, please. Travelers all, not
a single native, passport control's
nightmare: The woman from Zimbabwe
now lives in London and works for the scouts.
Newfoundlander in Slovenia who gave up
directing choirs, American not in Paris
but in Copenhagen, awaiting citizenship. Low
light, not quite candle-flicked
over the gathered, laughter fizzes
bubbly like Cava. Goblets filled, agua
mineral sin gas. Outside slab stone
walls, mazed narrow streets, wisps
of tobacco smoke curl up toward slim
swaths of inky sky. Inside, thin-sliced
Iberian ham melts on the tongue. Over ice,
in clear, heavy glasses, Monkey 47 gin
from the Black Forest, generously poured,
clinked in spontaneous cheers. In such company
alliances forge unlikely borders—dog owners,
circus lovers, an errant poet, survivors
of abandoned jobs without soul. Full-bodied
banter, a leisurely hum, no great expectations,

evening flip-flopping into the indigo hues
of nighttime proper, soon to part, disciples
of a peculiar sort. Gothic quarter made new
by craft food:
tiny ladles of cold mushroom soup
served in slender stemware,
platters of monkfish and prawns, paella
heaped into drifts. Bread shed from hot baked
loaves. Then the fellowship will scatter, stars
thrown as silver sequins against silk-black
skyline, into the cigarette and wine
and coffee smell that only Europe
holds dear. The passionfruit aperitif
is on the house.

Reviewer's Notes

Definitive account of nothing,
mundane's coup de gras, touch
of ordinary, pedantic, everyday:
red table wine & instant
oatmeal, fabulously outfitted
chicken nuggets, box-store
ambition, the sensible sedan
driven through suburbia, the cracker-
jack prize, full of nuts
and caramel, signifying little
league, my kid's an honors
student, over-stocked
candy canes left in January
crumbled into bits. It's television
upstairs & downstairs, dinner trays
of mac-n-cheese and crinkle-cut
fries from the frozen food isle.
No hand-crafted Italian loafers
but sensible sneakers with orthotic
inserts, purchased after filling out
a questionnaire at a kiosk between
anti-fungal gel and Band-aids. No
artifice or artisanal cheeses, just super-sized
diet drinks & mentholyptus
coating the throat in sugar
& syrup. The tickle, the catch, that scratchy
voice soothed into the otherworld

of home remedies and toaster strudel—
those tiny million busynothings, pressing in
and leaving us just a bit wrecked.

Sex Lives of Preppy Girls

Because I always wear these lustrous
pearls doesn't means I lack
other needs.

Why, today I perfectly mismatched my bra
and panties to coordinate exactly the Kelly
green and pink madras skirt. I'll give you
one guess as to which one is pink.

I like men the same way I drink scotch—
neat. Or occasionally on the rocks. Why
do you think I've straddled ponies
all these years?

I've been told I have a lovely seat.

A little sand in my Keds never hurt
me. Clam bakes, lobster boils,
or, let's just suck the oyster from the shell.

Aren't you even the tiniest bit curious about
what else might be monogramed?

Not all bows and champagne bubbles,
and god knows what
I'm taking in behind the polarized lenses
of these wayfarers.

Pack a picnic lunch, in wicker basket.
Together, we'll wind a country lane
in an antique roadster. Do me a favor?

As much as I love the retrievers, let's
leave them at home. And yes—

The pearls always stay on.

Winter Solstice

I was born
the darkest night of the year.

Mom says,
every day after me filled with more light.

But Mom,
what if I prefer the dark?

In the light
these eyes sometimes deceive me,

lack
of sight a kind of vision.

Better to trust
my fast-beating heart. Winters

in West Virginia
run unpredictable. Seventy degrees

during Valentine's
& snow in April, just like the Prince song.

How did we
lose our way? The tall pines shudder—

a howling wind
echoes through the frost like a lost friend.

My bones
prefer the chill of winter to summer's heat,

& my face,
tingling from cold, great puffs

I might swallow back whole.

Like a Lion, Like a Lamb

This is the part
where you say
"It was never like this."
Except

it always was. The rain
in West Virginia falls
as much as Seattle, maybe
more. Today wet-green & cold
only March would provide.

It could always turn slush, snow.

You say, "No," even as I refuse
to believe it. The dog's golden
fur caked in loose mud, shed
in long lines around the house.
The rain

a tickle throughout the day,
slow hours until they've tumbled
into night. This is the part

where you say,

"You were never like this."

Except

I always have been, exactly this:
steady rain that turns slushy,
a temporary snow right before the buds
push out from the branches.

Postcard Falling from an Unnamed Waterfall at the Edge of the Amazon Basin

Whoosh—
rush of water
perched on a boulder
after hiking the winding path
through massive ferns
and fronds
canopy of leaves shading
the journey.
Constant fall and flow
and me
so still
tiny
like the yellow or pink
flowers cloistered
in the massive quilt work
of green,
the ones you miss
unless you stop,
look. You missed
me, or it, or both.
Whoosh. We are calling.

Love Letters

Last night I dreamt of you
faraway, not in this city
hemmed-in streets, the pinks
and periwinkles, meringue edged buildings.
The mountains are taller, undulating
swell and dip, a feeling
you might recognize
The sweet papaya of morning,
noon's savory potatoes, gooey
cheese empanadas, tastes
you cannot know.
Sun blinding the eyes, pinks the skin.
Back home, summer rains,
a grayed sky where here it reigns blue.
Could you imagine me,
perched on a river rock
in the cool spray of water tumbling
towards some unknown destination?
I traveled across a deep ravine
in a metal basket, & back again.
Back again, we see the wonder, return
with stories in our hearts, hoping we
might faithfully recall this tale, but like love,
we only show our best approximation.
Could I weave together
the sound of strumming,
flap of bright flag,

snap of chili in the chocolate? And you?
The days I know and don't,
clouds in wait behind the mountain
obscure our vistas, across
continents I find what I already know.
Correspond with thorns wrapped
around our lonely tick-tock hearts.
Instead I send this postcard from
a dusty box at earth's shifting center,
a memory kiss this heart's postscript.

Dream Cycle 44

In the Sonoran Desert
mountains never quite close,
never too far away, loom
over a dusty valley, spiky plants,
rock, hummingbirds as colorful
as peacocks. How is it
mountains always find me?
No shifting sands, the sun warms the rock
warms the snake. Birds
roost in a saguaro. The peaks pierce
December clouds and make rain.
Tomorrow the sun returns from hiatus,
the moonlight glints off needles and glass,
and sleep comes swift, deep despite
howls, maybe from coyote, or people in lap
pool waves, their ice melting in a tumbler
full of nothings and half prayers and fire-water
and despair. The valley twinkles artificial
light, bleats like an out-of-tune cornet. Pomegranates
and chilies thick on the branch, whir of HVAC, forty-
four cycles came before.

Postcards Sent to El Quatre Gats

Pablo—
sometimes you ruin
me, your blue and your rose,
illness or circus, dwarf
and mother. Gone: communion,
science and charity. But the roofs
of Barcelona all azure angular
seascape. I miss
your golden pooch. Reality dissolved:
after the remote Pyrenes
you displayed your wares in New York.
Essence is what we're all after
after all. In Montparnasse, among
harlequins and whores, the world geometric
explodes in parallelograms of
garish color.

Olga—
Perhaps you should have stayed
with Ballet Russe. The faun, the spring
full of rites, Petrushka's doll. After Diaghilev,
didn't you see the Minotaur coming?
Iconography reveals what words
or love cannot. Pattern the psyche
surreal: a young mistress, fascism,
Guernica, not cross-eyed but eyes
fashioned in squat crosses,

Minotaur, Minotaur, the aberrant flying fish.

Gilot—
Can a villa between Cannes
and Antibes be enough? A house, only structure,
does not make a home, and the brilliance
cerulean can haunt your dreamland.
He will turn
to sculpture, later ceramics, embraces
Spanish baroque. He never turns to you,
Broken or otherwise shattered, not mosaic,
never a pivot you seek. Recognize
lonely heart bleats.

Jacqueline—
Overseer of Les Meninas,
and how did you like Senior Velazquez?
Did he suit your teatime, or do you drink dark
coffee? Champagne? Finally black, white, gray.
As if his brightness saved for pigeons, and you,
the intense blued seascape, hued solitude, a sleepy dog,
the bullfight, a backlit purity burnished by
brimstone and lechery, beginning and end
as if all creation, as if God himself
might be in on the joke.

Elegy

How strange a thing—
the loop-de-loop and curlicues.
L died a week ago Friday,
collaged until the end.
Don't cry in front of her Victorian War Paint,
cry alone. I didn't quite tell her
"goodbye." In that pause, I told her
I loved her. L wordless, skin yellowed
a hue in the dress of her robot-girl.
"A chaplain, a doctor,
& a poet walk into a hospital room..."
No punchline, but we laughed anyway,
diversion from her slipping. We could still smell
the glue, see a glint of light on silver scissors.
An interlocking moment of friendship between women,
that peculiar bloom like a bird of paradise. Then, only
the beep of the morphine drip, the slow descent
into sleep. We sang a Bob Dylan song—
the one she most liked and I never remember right.
She looked just like her robot-girls, until, of course
she didn't. We all have a heart
stitched on the outside of our frocks.

Postcard from the
Edge of the Amazon

My toucan had a blue face,
wary of people, searching for food,
mine only because he's the first
I've seen. At the wildlife preserve
birds squawk until fed, loud screeches
rising into the trees. The caimans
crashed the party, snuck in among
the turtles, not gated off. Barely
noticed us, rows of teeth and their tough
bumpy skin. Monkeys, an ocelot, just a taste
of the Amazon we skirted, flowers everywhere,
bright plumes against the deep
green. I can't imagine
all the animals like the toucan,
the funny squat bird.

Postcard Written at
My Brother's House

The best room in the house is the one
my brother's in. He has cancer. He has
his daughter tucked to his side, his long
legs splayed on the ottoman, torso
propped up on the couch. We cannot know
the outcome. Mom crochets a throw
in garnet and gold, his alma mater's
colors. The boys play on the floor in the half-
light of pulled blinds. Shadows cast on LEGOS
and remote-control cars. What is a house for?

Brick walls that will one day crumble,
mortar and drywall behind which
we gather, avoiding heat or rain, collecting backpacks
and junk mail, serving snacks or family feasts. Pickled-eggs,
our father's favorite. My brother, lean from chemo,
eats hummus and pretzels, drinks Arnold Palmers.
Still has his hair, dark flecked with silver. He has Mom's nose,
the shape of Dad's eyes. We

build our homes without knowing the pale-lit
future, just flimsy hopes, which feel important
And then, as if to wake, the high-pitched laughter of kids
tickled, making these walls with these windows, entries and exits,
more than a blueprint or a floor plan, more like a home.

Postcard Made of Taffy

Avenue alive, knots of people,
storefront-framed, a man
pulls a long length
of taffy, twists, lets out the tension,
pulls again. Couples arm
in arm, a single woman
carrying two over-filled bags.
Hum of motorbikes and aging
cars. Pink, aqua, yellow, green—
the colors of candy, the same colors infused
all over this country, ones I might remember
from South Florida, a time and place faded,
a reverse Polaroid, until the swirl, twirl
of the sweet shop's lollipops dissolve.
In Baños de Agua Santa, children
oblivious, run past, one with her hair
pulled into a tiny bun, a Minnie Mouse
backpack burdens her shoulders. The taffy man loops
the not yet candy around a hook, stops
chats up his friend, turns back, loops again.
Baños follows such taffy rhythms:
traffic tumbles past. Even the pigeons
in the center square, startled, take flight
swoop, land again. Back and forth
tension and slack, governed perhaps
by the labor of unmade candies.

Postcard Composed at Panadería

Polaca, sweet and cold
sipped as I sit, a nook &
cranny café, full of baked
wonder, wafting warmth of bread.
To eat such simple luxury,
words I've never known float
in an opera of ordinary. Last night,
I dreamt of my dog, her soft
golden fur. The dogs of Quito
trot by oblivious. Sometimes
they nap in the sun. We all have a place
we might belong. For now, I stare
at the bright-frosted cookies,
an emberglow of childhood,
considering their potential
sweetness.

Postcard from The Met

In the corner, as if forgotten
the mother with the stroller
stops, leans in.

A man with curls like a cherub,
freely attentive—

On canvas, an artist embraces
woman, his creation, legs
stony to the thigh that pinks
to life at the buttocks

supple at the spine

his firm grasp encircles her waist. Does
he think he might squeeze life into her?

The man with the cherub curls turns
as if to leave, twists back like Pygmalion
but startled.

Wide eyeing, me seated on the bench,
& within an eight count pivots,

glides into other exhibits—
when I lift my gaze, he's gone.

Shaken and Stirred

Today I dreamt of swimming,
the cool splash of water, diving in.
Outside, flurries dance on air or nothing,
backstrokes through a great unknown space.
That space is between us now, and I'm not
sure how it got there. I wonder might we
ride those flakes, cold and earthbound
but for this moment floating, delaying gravity,
defying all the things we've never said?
My heart's landscape has never been
the winter moon. Back on earth, the hum
of traffic, cool scrape of brakes, deliveries made,
beckoned by gravel driveways. The porch lights on,
snapped off. Leftovers not only fill
my fridge, but my heart too, that lonely organ
pumping in ceaseless clock-beats marking
time I have left. Maybe the world is a giant
snow globe, trapping our memories, those particulates
hurling down to settle on grass like salt
from the shaker. My heart will tumble its tiny
artificial flakes and sparkle
until they all find the ground. And then?
Maybe that shake and sparkle will have been enough.

For M, Pirouette

The depth of starlight equals your heartbeat
squared, that series of entrechat-quatres
and passés. The arrow to the moon a leggy
line of penché, pointe shoe cleaving
harvest glow. Not quite Clair de Lune.

The high inner lines, refracting
shadows cast by écarté. The un-light until
you move again. Crescent moon:
over the smatter of fresh snowfall,
each tiny, crystalline glitter-orb.

One day you will witness
the vast, dark sky, wonder
at the twirling pinpoint of light,
that spinning self I've seen.

Postcards from the Old World

The chocolate sold in bricks like looted
gold bars. That long-ago queen shipped
De Leon to the new world searching
for youth and fortune when it was here
all along. Shopkeep's question: English
or Spanish, Miss? If you have euros
or American Express, you
are open to largess. Placed
like a lozenge
or communion wafer,
on my tongue, prelude
to prayer. Flavored so
decadent, one might say opulent,
deep cocoa, not too sweet.
Europe's surprise:
chocolate tastes deep
Mediterranean blue.

Bluegrass Kitchen

The robin's eggshell blue
of an era passed
repurposed as hostess station.
Tin-tiled roof, imperfect, peeled
in places, as if to say age
could be a good thing, history
ongoing, alive, jive piped
over the speaker. The bright red
Fiestaware a nod, loyal
West Virginians. This dreamland
faces the boarded-up husk
of commerce. Fries salted,
vinegar-malted, melt
on fingers & tongue. Late-day
sun filters in the storefront,
vintage RESTAURANT sign
unlit but glowing. Home brews.
Coffee. The rattle of a rusting
Escort ambling down the street.
Part of me from a lost past
I half remember.

Ave Maria

The saints are busy in Baños
after the mortals cleanse
in the virgin's protective waters
saving the tourist from the car
tumbling towards the river,
or
the volcano
erupting in hot scarlet and ash.
The turquoise and gold overhead,
bit of red, like all sanctuaries in Ecuador,
a golden pulpit, as if all the wealth
heaved itself into the dominion
of heavenly fathers. My eyes strain
against such splendor, the art fearsome allegories,
the din of foreign-tongued incantations echo
in the great domes overhead. Prayer,
mediation, remembering how small
I am, how much I might never explain.
Please, Saints, spare a glance in my direction.
When I raise my eyes, the virgin holds
a skewered heart in her hand, the angel
pierces the deep-burned devils. But Jesus
looks bored, gazes right at me.
The tight rope walker survives
even as his line breaks.

Pop Life

Sexy dancer, all the critics love you
in New York. Around the world
in one day, rave un2 the joy fantastic—
breakfast can wait. Way back home,
when doves cry, do it all night. In
this bed I scream, "nothing compares
2 U." When you were mine, I would
die 4 U. Ain't about to stop: Pink
cashmere, housequake, cream, purple rain.

Vacationland

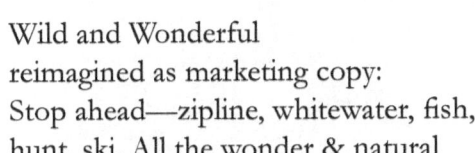

Wild and Wonderful
reimagined as marketing copy:
Stop ahead—zipline, whitewater, fish,
hunt, ski. All the wonder & natural
beauty. Book now:

don't mind that smell,
no acid mine drainage here, no
chemicals scented licorice, which you can buy
in the boutique. Mine's been closed these many

years. Topless mountains, naked,
unashamed. Reclaimed,
leveled perfectly for your family picnic
red gingham table cloth, basket filled,
no pesky trees to block your sun. Bathe
in our light. Escape your reality—we'll make do
with minimum wage & Medicaid, if
it all works out. Leave behind the hawkers,
gawkers, seekers of poverty porn. We're
beyond that now, we're greened and open—

our whitewashed past repackaged
for your amusement: feuds,
moonshine, mineshafts. Make
your reservation. We plant
our pretty scene, stop for scenic views,

a postcard to remember us when you're packed
& gone. Stacks of spent bills line the pocket
of a man in some other state, same
as it ever was. Never you mind.
Ya'll come back now! Our door
flung wide, as if your vacation
might save us.

The Gilded Sanctuary

After dark, we climbed the cobbled streets
up the steep incline as music poured out
from cafés and cantinas, rolling into the cool
of night and tumbling downhill.
In today's light, a church so ornate
gold ceases to be a color, becomes an aura.
Isaiah stares out, imploring us to wait
upon the Lord for wings as eagles
while Ezekiel looks past—
we are not here for him. Then, Judas,
downcast sideways eye
as if he knows some secret sin
I harbor deep inside. The martyred
woman, sainted, swaddled in black behind glass
as if only she deserves such direct viewing.
Her black more than the absence
of color. Above, a priest wields the cross
over the dark, kneeling child. But will he
save him? My pew, hard, ornate
facing the glow of an altar
long after its use. Perhaps Judas
will leave his frame, climb the pulpit
and find voice to sing. So much
gold can only lead to song.
Down the long stretch of the sanctuary's
center stands a solitary shepherd boy,
his flock a solitary lamb.

No number of angels or saints
could save us this much. Before
tour's end I visit Judas
a last time, ready, I suppose,
to return to the gaudy and weary
world, ready for the next
wonder. Tonight, we might wander
back to the cantina, the music,
the world not of gold or saints
but sinners and lust and laughter,
this dreamland an invitation to bask
both in dark and in the light.

Year of the Rooster

Imagine the tractor supply
selling fluffy yellow chicks
choosing four, all of which
turn out to be roosters.

Every other house along the blocks
line their yards with signs:
competing candidates. Contrary
to popular belief, roosters crow

at times other than daybreak,
their primal caw piercing the night,
the mid-afternoon when people work
or nap or take tea. Each morning

I walk a trail, the kind Austen might have
penned as a pretty bit of wilderness. I take
my turn in it, quiet so thick
only the thunderous rustle

of leaves. By the reservoir
an old metal chair, water unfit
to swim in, shadowed by cloud-cover,
devoid of roosters, of signs, yet flanked

by autumnglow soon to surrender.

Dear Nate: Midday Amsterdam

Even the dimmed lamppost, efficient
yet old, whispers the past. Fat
pigeons parade low grade roofs.
Grasses in a planter bow
to the wind. The ramshackle
feel of some canals remind me
of a home I can't quite
conjure up. Rickety chairs
occupied by women in black, elegant,
smoking over cupped coffee, their faraway
stares and wispy hair make me wonder
if they're thinking of someone
dear, departed, just as the wrinkles
and graying hair began to show—

maybe like I am thinking of you,
and then you are gone. The wind ruffles up
and the stone path underfoot. How many cities
shall I see if never with you? Slant glow,
Northern Europe, dying
colors of the houseboats lining canals—
your shadow self, stuck
at age forty-two.

Night vision: in Holland
late year dusk falls at four,
lampposts echo past light. Quiet waterways

lead nowhere but around. Eager tourists
glide over the surface looking towards
history in the bricks of buildings, the tall windows,
as if the dead reveal their secrets like artificial light.

Joy/Infusion Clinic

I sat with truck drivers and bus drivers and heavy equipment operators. A real railroader. Ladies who picnic in graveyards. The law clerk. The makers of bread and fried chicken. I sat in awe of the McDonald's shift manager, laid off coal miner, the small town loan officer whose bank finances first cars and first homes and college educations, dreams bigger and better than the drip bag tethered to the insert port of entry. I sat with their spooled-out stories: horseshoe champions, shootings, Christmas dinners, cruises to Egypt, the boy on the bus who only trusted the driver when he was alone and scared and unable to cope. The sweet swell of music and wind. They open their dusty treasure-trove of lore, loves, fears, their deep-bellied laughs, the wayward tear apologized for when no apology was necessary. I sat with the woman whose true love loved horses, with the dog rescuers, the proud owners of a pot-bellied pig named Miss Piggy. Some survived and others survived on paper, taking up residence in my heart, when I breathe or eat or walk or love. A part of them twines up in some part of me—maybe I learned how to listen—and find their way in my scribbles years later. I sat with the living, the soon dead. When I speak of the dead, like my brother, I don't whisper, but break open as if in song.

Tracing Inert Gasses on West Virginia Day

Truth is, I don't really know
what xenon is, but some nights
full up with stars, summer sky
might just be packed with satellites,
planets, or some kind of space
junk, twinkling away as if it wasn't
flotsam from the Space Race, husks
of men's egos past needing to tame
heaven. Here, in this place, lightning bugs
also known as fireflies illuminate a second
before moving on. I'm living in this time
where the watch around my wrist
tends not to keep much meaning. I saw
a baby groundhog slip into a drain;
groundhogs are also known as woodchucks or
whistle pigs, these words so slippery I can't
seem to hold on to any, can't grasp
their meanings, as if all the words
that might explain this one moment in time
all morphed into glittering space junk, orbiting,
spinning madly around us, spinning
madly until this day, when a state
was born, not inert like xenon, but out
of conflict which flashes its underbelly
not whistle pig or lightning bug or any other
synonym that's not quite the right word. Garbage
stars float in the night sky among those that implode
into a great, gaping nothing. A black hole

swallowed up God. Yet wonder
refuses being inert or being snuffed out.

Questions of Understanding

Status quo ex ante
& yawn, the bare room, giant
screen, efficient stadium seating
as if slotted, as if the mind sanitized
might be more productive. Could you
imagine the wind over water, a canal?
The low light of autumn in north country
more than the collective hum of agreement,
nods as if here is where it's at. Outside
the wind we cannot hear should remind us
of all we might not contain.

Dear Nate: Concourse

Miffy the bunny glows in the red light
of Amsterdam's airport, not quite the carnal
delight one expects. It's not Miffy's fault.
The cannabis lollipops can be had
in the shops of this plein or that. Here
the efficient bustle of duty free & passport control—
planes & gates & us weary travelers flung
this way & that through the sky
that hung a moon & stars over all of us, even
Miffy, even me, lone wanderer, searching
this world for what I lost back home.

How to See This Empty, I Look

Mostly
I see dust motes
or the nothing
we call air and breathe, cluttered
particulates and all. Cut
between this
light and that, I imagine
a you-shaped
hole: the curve of
your calf that's like
the curve of my calf, replica
of the curve
of our mother's calf and
I wonder how genes
work until the whir
of someone's lawnmower
snaps me back to the eaves
of my house, casting
shadows on the grass, greener
in the shade or
maybe this heart sees
where the light lingers,
cylinders of hope and
dust as if ashes might
fly up and become stars. What
star are you? Caught
in half joy-sorrows, forever

this year, and also just a blink?
Blink.
Light.

Dear Nate: Plantages

The Chinese restaurant empty, as if
no one needed to eat for days. A man
speaking agitated, impossible
language of doubled-vowels
and guttural words. I found another
back way, so pleased as I pass new building
next to old, a paperback of translations jostling
in my bag. Brother, you are dead as part of me
struggles to keep alive. I forget the new reading
glasses, words blurring, double A's become four
become one, and then
nothing—
a smear of black. Even if I could
erase all the language, missing you presses
my wanderlust heart. The pub will warm with gathered
bodies, the golden beer glows in the pale light. Outside
the snap of evening chill, the smell of cigarettes against
the cold, against whatever it is that pulls us into night,
air heavy in our feeble chests, as if our breath might
be too much. As if, Brother, I might send my tiny
northern wind direct to you.

Aria, First Ward

I've begun to question
my insides out, the dog
and me on the cool patio

the felled remains of a dead
tree, some wood like sand

some tawny short planks
that might crackle, lit, fire

sunglow, from behind a hazy
cloud. Opaque. A kind of amber

buzz and hum of bee and bird
creatures that know what
they're about. My hows

and whys are out of joint,
a buzzing concerto
lawnmowers
among a standstill world lurching
through spring. Today I adorned

myself in jewelry just for me
and the dog. Who knows? Maybe
she appreciates such gesture

the normalcy of turquoise
and opal, and silver, stones
and metal not so precious

and if I am honest, the only
one to notice, perhaps
finally
     that's enough.

Storm Front, West Virginia

*--in this year of pandemonium, 2020
without hindsight.*

And here uneasy clouds shift
across otherwise blue-hued sky
burdened, gray, weary travelers
full of unspilled tears

or maybe I'm projecting and should be
happier, a sweet golden dog napping
at my feet

What's in the air can
kill you, says the scientist
    the preacher
    the doctor
    the politician

Above us, ghost armies claiming recruits
at an alarming clip, riding fast-moving
cloud cover, speeding over my little slope
destination known only to

    deities
    and fickle wind currents

a sky knowing what we might

never discover. Strands of hair
whip across my cheek, while the dog
raises her nose as if
to sniff what's coming.

Because Rest Was Once a Creative Act

Nestle down
    into that sweet spot
        of the night.
mint clinging
    to your brushed teeth
head heavy on the pillow
    where
    the deep thoughts of
        the poets
        have yet to morph
        into verse
Tremble-thoughts of days
    swirl with terrible
    velocity,
becoming billowy dreamstuff
and maybe tumbling
    over a green, downy bluff
where your windswept hair lashes
    exposed skin. Minty
    taste lingers on your tongue
a foreign language.
If you find yourself in the dissolve
    of tall grasses on the edge
        of that sinking horizon
so pink
so blue

Or the sleep sound of your lover
    keeps you tethered.
Topside. This warm bed.

Pickled Eggs

Probably I knew the root
popped up from the dirt
in just that place my toe
caught it. Body pitched
forward until gravity
pulled me groundward.
The impact ricocheted
through my bones. Stunned.
I felt the good dirt between
skin and fingernail. I sat
a moment, breath caught
somewhere in my windpipe,
fear of falling and the prospect
of getting up again comingled,
suspended time. But the trail
waited. Wind blew over the silenced
gravel. Later, I spooned up the purple
oval from the tall cylinder jar,
pungent, glistening, the golden shock
yolk at its center. Sweet tang from days
in that vinegar base, beets lending
color, preserved that moment as bruises
formed, mapping my fall, blooming
on the pale parchment of my skin,
a cartographer's fever dream, uncharted
counties along my dermis, while I fed
my hunger with the food of my recent

ancestors who lived in more hillscape
than me. Outside the cloud clover kept
close to the earth, winding down a path
where I'd walk again and again, a creature
of place and habit.

Doctor, Doctor

You've seen them: the hearts,
fingers curved and thumbs straight—
the vials in the Doctor's hands,
a heart, cleaved in two, pierced.
What does Doctor see?
The worn mask has been hopelessly
cleaned, used until the using
makes it useless. When Doctor gets
to eat an apple a day, will he get a taste
response, or is that gone, too? The hand heart steady—
what if Doctor is just a person, with a job,
with kids, hopes, a spouse, a mortgage,
fears, a dog to run, earbuds
full of showtunes and podcasts. This Doctor
is every doctor. In a cosmic instant,
he watches the world tumble to the ICU tune:
whirs and chirrs and beeps and clanks,
symphony by the suffering. But we all
suffer, and no one knows that better. Doctor, heal
me and perhaps also be healed. Hypnotic
stare, decoding a message through safety goggles
fogged, the soft pad of good-soled shoes
on linoleum, green-tinged fluorescents
overhead, in the day-night, or night-day.
Who can tell? Time's a concept
all used up. Message in a bottle:
Doctor, don't despair. Just look. Daffodils

raise their bright yellow heads
even as you leave, dead hour in the dark,
heart-hands clasped around the steering wheel,
instinct guiding you home.

Postscript (for you)

Moon skin, bird song,
smell of eucalyptus,
rhythmic footfalls &
in the deep chocolate
on my tongue, my thoughts
drift to you. The hot day &
the cold cerveza I know
you'd enjoy. Under the canopy
of trees I remember
the sly smiles of the locals
the weight of the word foreign.
At night, I dream of dancing,
moon skin catching light
from a thousand stars, and wings
I might fly. Tears, gushing over
the undulating waterfall, all the weeping
I have yet to do cascading from the high peak.
Me, a pilgrim upon the cobblestone path,
I do not stumble.

Acknowledgments

Grateful acknowledgement to the following publications where poems from this collection originally appeared: "Postcards to West Virginia," "Winter Solstice," and "Like a Lion, Like a Lamb" in A Poetry Congeries at Connotation Press; "Zen Cancer Saloon," "Dreamland," and "Eucalyptus" in Triggerfish Critical Review; "Curtain Call" in Still: A Journal; "Boy Killed on the Grafton Road" in The Anthology of Appalachian Writers and Eyes Glowing at the Edge of the Woods; "Bury the Lead" in Bellevue Literary Review; "For M, Pirouette" in Heartwood Literary Magazine; "Tracing Inert Gasses on West Virginia Day" in Dead Mule School of Southern Literature; "Joy/Infusion Clinic" and "Because Rest Was Once a Creative Act" in WANA Journal. The following poems were included in the Women of Appalachia Project's Women Speak performances in 2017-2018: "Zen Cancer Saloon," "Eucalyptus," "Boy Killed on the Grafton Road," and "Dreamland."

Renée K. Nicholson is the author of Fierce and Delicate: Essays on Dance and Illness, co-editor of the award-winning anthology Bodies of Truth: Personal Narratives of Illness, Disability, and Medicine, and the poetry collection Roundabout Directions to Lincoln Center. She directed the Humanities Center at West Virginia University until 2024, and is a creative partner in Healthcare Is Human, a nonprofit dedicated to authentic storytelling in healthcare. Renée is a contributing writer for Synapsis: a Journal of Health Humanities, and the author of many creative pieces and scholarly articles. Renée was a past Emerging Writer-in-Residence at Penn State-Altoona, and the recipient of the 2018 Susan S. Landis Award for Distinguished Service to the Arts from the West Virginia Division of Arts, Culture, and History.